THE LITTLE BOOK OF
AWAKENING

THE LITTLE BOOK OF AWAKENING

52 Weekly Selections

MARK NEPO

Red Wheel

This edition first published in 2024 by Red Wheel,
an imprint of
Red Wheel/Weiser, LLC
With offices at:
65 Parker Street, Suite 7
Newburyport, MA 01950
www.redwheelweiser.com

Copyright © 2000, 2013 by Mark Nepo.
Introduction to this edition copyright © 2013.

All rights reserved. No part of this publication
may be reproduced or transmitted in any form or
by any means, electronic or mechanical, including
photocopying, recording, or by any information storage
and retrieval system, without permission in writing
from Red Wheel/Weiser, LLC. Reviewers may quote
brief passages. This edition is excerpted from *The Book
of Awakening*, first published by Conari Press in 2000,
ISBN: 978-1-57324-117-5.

ISBN: 978-1-59003-540-5

Library of Congress Cataloging-in-Publication data
available upon request

Cover design by Kathryn Sky-Peck
Interior by Maureen Forys, Happenstance
Type-O-Rama

Printed in the United States of America
IBI
10 9 8 7 6 5 4 3 2 1

Introduction to the
Little Book of Awakening

These weekly selections are taken from my spiritual daybook, *The Book of Awakening,* which was first published in 2000. Like any author, I've been changed by what has come through me, and this book continues to be my teacher. I first explored and gathered these pages freshly on the other side of cancer, when I was gentle and raw and eager to give something back. Since that time, the book has had a remarkable journey. It's been translated into more than twenty languages and is now in its 31st printing. It's all very humbling.

I must say that surviving cancer taught me that we're not here just to pay the bills and cross off tasks on our never-ending lists. In the midst of all the effort it takes to survive, we each need the gift of wakefulness in order to thrive. In truth, what matters—what keeps us alive and close to joy—is always nearby, hidden in the folds of whatever trouble or detour we trip on. With this in mind, this edition is intended to be small enough to carry with you, an in-hand companion. It is my hope that you'll find something here to calm, comfort, challenge, and stretch you, and most of all to introduce you to yourself.

—MARK, SEPTEMBER 2013

THE LITTLE BOOK OF AWAKENING

Burning the Wrapper

From the beginning,
The key to renewal has been shedding,
The casting off of old skin.

The Polynesians say the world began when Taaora—their name for the Creator—woke to find himself growing inside a shell. He stretched and broke the shell, and the Earth was created. Taaora kept growing, though, and after a time found himself inside another shell. Again, he stretched and broke the shell, and this time the moon was created. Again, Taaora kept growing, and again, he found himself contained by yet another shell. This time the breaking forth created the stars.

In this ancient story, the Polynesians have carried for us the wisdom that we each grow in this life by breaking successive shells, that the piece of God within each of us stretches until there's no room to be, and then the world as we know it must be broken so that we can be born anew.

In this way, life becomes a living of who we are until that form of self can no longer hold us, and, like Taaora in his shell, we must break the forms that contain us in order to birth our way into the next self. This is how we shed our many ways of seeing the world, not that any are false, but that each serves its purpose for a time until we grow and they no longer serve us.

I have lived through many selves. The first of me, so eager to be great, to set things ablaze, shunned everything that was ordinary. I hunted the burn of a champion's hip and wanted to be a great musician too—to be famous and extraordinary. But as I grew, the notion of fame left me lonely in the night. Thrones, no matter how pretty, have only room for one.

The second of me wanted to be covered by waves, inhale the stars, and move like a song. Now I wanted to be the great music itself. But to be the great thing was still as lonely as it was magnificent.

The third of me gave up on greatness. It was how I let others draw close. I asked more questions, not really interested in answers, but more, the face below the face about to speak.

And then during cancer, there came yet another self—there, bent and distorted in the hospital chrome as the late sun flooded my pillow. I was dead in the chrome, alive on the pillow, a quiet breath between—dead, alive—at once. And oddly, it did not scare, for I felt the pulse of life in the quiet breath, and the place to which I transcended is here.

Almost dying was another shell I had to break. It has led me to realize that each self unfolds, just one concentric womb en route to another, each encompassing the last. I would believe in arrival but for all the arrivals I've broken on the way.

- ○ *Breathe slowly with your eyes closed, and feel one aspect of your current world that seems confining.*

- ○ *Rather than focusing on the people or circumstance involved, try to feel this confinement as the threshold of your next growth.*

○ *Meditate on how the piece of God within you might stretch and stand more fully, so that being who you are more completely will break the shell of this confinement.*

○ *Pray to understand that none of this is bad, but simply necessary for the growth of your soul.*

The Art of Facing Things

> What people have forgotten is what
> every salmon knows.
> —ROBERT CLARK

Salmon have much to teach us about the art of facing things. In swimming up waterfalls, these remarkable creatures seem to defy gravity. It is an amazing thing to behold. A closer look reveals a wisdom for all beings who want to thrive.

What the salmon somehow know is how to turn their underside—from center to tail—into the powerful current coming at them, which hits them squarely, and the impact then launches them out and further up the waterfall; to which their reaction is, again, to turn their underside back into the powerful current that, of course, again hits them squarely; and this successive impact launches them further out and up the waterfall. Their leaning into what they face bounces them further and further along their unlikely journey.

From a distance, it seems magical, as if these mighty fish are flying, conquering their element. In actuality, they are deeply at one with their element, vibrantly and thoroughly engaged in a compelling dance of turning-toward-and-being-hit-squarely that moves them through water and air to the very source of their nature.

In terms useful to the life of the spirit, the salmon are constantly faithful in exposing their underside to the current coming at them. Mysteriously, it is the physics of this courage that enables them to move through life as they know it so directly. We can learn from this very active paradox; for we, too, must be as faithful to living in the open if we are to stay real in the face of our daily experience. In order not to be swept away by what the days bring, we, too, must find a way to lean into the forces that hit us so squarely.

The salmon offer us a way to face truth without shutting down. They show us how leaning into our experience, though we don't like the hit, moves us on. Time and again, though we'd rather turn away, it is the impact of being revealed, through our willingness to be vulnerable, that enables us to experience both mystery and grace.

○ *Sit quietly and meditate on the last time you opened yourself to the life coming at you.*

○ *In recalling this, try to focus on three things: the way that opening yourself caused you to unfold, the way that being hit squarely changed your life position, and where leaping like a salmon landed you.*

○ *Breathe steadily, and invite the lessons of opening, being changed, and landing into your heart.*

○ *Breathe slowly, and realize that you are in this process now.*

○ *Relax and turn the belly of your heart toward the day.*

Compassion

I have just three things to teach:
simplicity, patience, compassion.
These are your greatest treasures.
Compassionate toward yourself,
you reconcile all beings in the world.

—LAO-TZU

A t first, we might ask, How can being compassionate to yourself reconcile all beings in the world?

To understand the gift of this, we need to recall the analogy of the Spoked Wheel, in which each life is a separate and unique spoke, and yet all lives, like those spokes, meet in a common hub or center. That's why when we tend our deepest center, we care for all souls.

Another powerful way to realize our interconnectedness is to imagine the human family as a stand of aspens growing by a river. Though each tree appears to be growing independently, not attached to the others, beneath the soil, out of view, the roots of all the trees exist as one enormous root. And so, like these trees, our soul's growth, while appearing to be independent, is intimately connected to the health of those around us. For our spirits are entwined at center, out of view.

Once realizing this, it becomes clear that we have no choice but to embrace the health of our neighbors as part of our own health. I felt this deeply in the many cancer rooms I sat in. I know these things to be true: in cutting off strangers, we cut off ourselves; in choking roots, we choke our own growth; in loving strangers, we love ourselves.

Having come this far, I believe that Lao-Tzu's third instruction tells us that if we are aware of our own suffering with the wish to relieve it, we will overcome distrust and reestablish a close relationship with all other living things. In deep and lasting ways, when we heal ourselves, we heal the world. For as the body is only as healthy as its individual cells, the world is only as healthy as its individual souls.

Across the centuries, we have this timeless medicine: Live directly, wait, and care for your soul as if it were the whole world.

○ *Breathe slowly, and feel your heart constrict and dilate as your eyes do.*

○ *Breathe slowly, and care for your soul with each breath. Feel your heart expand. Feel your sense of self open.*

○ *Breathe slowly, and feel your sense of the world open as you care for your soul.*

Love at First Sight

Where two deliberate, the love is slight.
Whoever loved, not having loved
at first sight.

—CHRISTOPHER MARLOWE

The true power of love at first sight is often missed because we insist on limiting its meaning to the sweep of falling into another person upon first meeting. To appreciate the deeper sense of this, we must uncover and reclaim the importance of first sight itself, which has more to do with seeing things essentially, rather than physically, for the first time.

We all walk around within the numbness of our habits and routines so often that we take the marvels of ordinary life for granted. It is first sight that opens the freshness of each moment, unencumbered by any of our habits and routines. First sight is the moment of God-sight, heart-sight, soul-sight. It is the seeing of revelation, the feeling of oneness that briefly overcomes us when nothing remains in the way.

At its deepest and most real level, the notion of love at first sight is spoken of in every spiritual tradition as the reward for being fully awake. Such seeing anew restores our sense of being alive. Paradoxically, first sight is recurring. In the same way that we wake every day, we regularly return to first sight in the rhythm of our wakefulness of spirit. Whenever we can see with that original vision—with nothing between us and the life around us—we can't help but love what we see. To see so fundamentally opens us to love. To love so fundamentally is to see the world we're a part of as the vibrant, ongoing creation that it is. So, it really manifests this way: at first sight, we find love; at our first true seeing, the love that is already there touches us.

In this regard, first seeing is an ever-present threshold to the majesty of what is. Certainly and beautifully, this happens with other people when we, upon first truly seeing another, fall sweetly into the miracle of their presence. But this is also possible, on a daily basis, upon first truly seeing ourselves, our world, our sense of God—again and again.

I can work across from the same person for years, and one day, because my own suffering has opened me more fully than I can remember and because the light floods that person's face, I can for the first time truly see who they are and feel love for them. I can walk by the same willow, season after season, and one day, because of the sheen of after-rain and the lowness of the wind, I can truly see the willow like never before, and feel love for the willow in all of us. I can, in the mirror late at night, after seeing myself hundreds of times, see the willow and the light and the other in my tired face, and know that sameness as the stuff of God.

In truth, it has never been about first meeting, though this can happen, but more about first coming into view. As a breeze all spun out lets the water go clear, we finally stop talking, stop performing, stop pretending, and all tired out, we go clear, and the heart that rests in everything beats before us.

○ *Close your eyes and breathe away your mind-sight, your*

past-sight, your future-sight, your wounded-sight.

○ With each slow breath, feel the cool air of your birth-sight, your first-sight.

○ Breathe slowly and imagine that the beat of your heart carries up the beginning-of-time-sight.

○ At the moment that you feel original, however briefly, open your eyes and bow with love to the first thing you see.

The Taste of Sky

Of magic doors there is this,
you do not see them even
as you are passing through.

—ANONYMOUS

Often as we are being transformed, we cannot tell what is happening. For while in the midst of staying afloat, it is next to impossible to see the ocean we are being carried into. While struggling with the pain of change, it is often impossible to see the new self we are becoming. While feeling our hand pried loose by experience, we seldom can imagine what will fill it once it is opened. As the days rinse our heart, we can feel something unseeable scour us through, though we can't yet imagine how much fresher milk and sky and laughter will taste once we are returned to the feel of being new.

○ *Sit quietly and bring to mind a struggle you are now experiencing in your life.*

○ *Breathe through this struggle and bless the buried part of you just waiting for its turn in the world.*

Against Our Will

As an inlet cannot close itself to the sea
that shapes it, the heart can only wear
itself open.

One of the hardest blessings to accept
about the heart is that in the image
of life itself, it will not stop emerging
through experience. No matter how we
try to preserve or relive what has already
happened, the heart will not stop being
shaped.

This is a magnificent key to health:
that, despite our resistance to accept
that what we've lost is behind us, despite
our need at times to stitch our wounds

closed by reliving them, and despite our heroic efforts to preserve whatever is precious, despite all our attempts to stop the flow of life, the heart knows better. It knows that the only way to truly remember or stay whole is to take the best and worst into its tissue.

Despite all our intentions not to be hurt again, the heart keeps us going by moving us ever forward into health. Though we walk around thinking we can direct it, our heart is endlessly shaped like the land, often against our will.

○ *Center yourself, and bring to mind one precious moment you'd like to preserve.*

○ *As you breathe, let in the life that is presently around you—the quality of light, the temperature, the sounds coming and going.*

○ *Breathe steadily and try not to choose one over the other. Simply allow the precious memory and the precious moment to tenderly become one.*

The Way Is Hard, but Clear

Though it is the hardest going,
the way is clear.

The naturalist and environmentalist Kevin Scribner tells us that salmon make their way upstream by bumping repeatedly into blocked pathways until they find where the current is strongest. Somehow they know that the unimpeded rush of water means that there is no obstacle there, and so they enter this opening fervently, for though it is the hardest going, the way is clear.

The lesson here is as unnerving as it is helpful. In facing both inner and outer adversities, the passage of truth comes at us with a powerful momentum because it is clear and unimpeded, and so, where we sense the rush of truth is where we must give our all.

As human beings, the blocked pathways of our journey can take on many forms, and—whether it be in avoiding conflict with others, or in not taking the risk to love, or in not accepting the call of spirit that would have us participate more fully in our days—it is often easier to butt up continually against these blocked pathways than to enter fervently the one passage that is so powerfully clear.

In this regard, salmon innately model a healthy persistence by showing us how to keep nosing for the unimpeded way, and once finding it, how to work even harder to make it through.

Some say it is easier for salmon, since the power of their drive to end where they begin is not compromised by the endless considerations that often keep us from the truth. Still, it is the heart's capacity to rise one more time after falling down, no matter how bruised, that verifies that such a drive lives in us too. Like salmon, our way depends not just on facing things head on, but in moving our whole being through.

○ *Center yourself and bring to mind something you are avoiding. It might be making a life decision or asking for what you need in a relationship.*

○ *Breathe evenly and nose around the energy of the avoidance. What are you butting up against? Identify the resistance. Which part is*

*coming from you? Which part
from others?*

○ *Breathe steadily and look for the
rush of truth in all this. Feel for
the clear and forceful way coming
at you.*

○ *For today, simply feel the power
of the way that is clear and keep it
before you.*

While Running

To see takes time.

—GEORGIA O'KEEFFE

While running in May, I saw a neatly trimmed hedge, and sprouting briskly through its symmetry were scraggly blue flowers wildly obeying no form. It made me smile, for I have spent many years resisting being pruned and shaped. I loved how the wild blue just hung there above the hedge.

While running in June, I saw an older man out pruning that hedge. He was so involved: clipping gingerly, then backing up, sweating through his eyes, as if the world depended on his diligence. I was touched by his care. He nodded briefly, and without a word, it was clear that it wasn't the hedge, but that he needed something to care for. I realized this is how I've lived since surviving cancer.

While running in August, I came upon a slim fountain gushing from an unseeable center, as high as it could, reaching without arms until it ran out of reach, and at its closest to the sky, it began to fall back on itself, always what was rising up replacing what was falling away. Sweating and heaving, I realized this is what it means to be free.

○ *Sit quietly, and call to the part in you that resists beings pruned. Affirm it.*

○ *Breathe deeply, and call to the part in you that needs to care. Embrace it.*

29

○ *Breathe feely, and call to the part*
in you that after reaching falls
back on itself. Bless it.

Beyond All Asking

If you try to understand love
before being held,
you will never feel compassion.

There was a boy who knew how to
make others relax by his friendly
talk, and once they relaxed, he'd ask
his many questions. But he always went
home alone. The next day he'd talk some
more, and sooner or later, he would
always get to questions of love, colorful
questions that would stretch and spread
and fall, just like leaves.

He lived this way for many years and
the deep asking opened his heart. The

space of his heart grew very wide and people would come and go like birds in the orchard of questions that was his heart. But once everyone left, he was alone with all he knew.

One day there was a vibrant being who would not enter the orchard of his questions. No matter how friendly he was, she wouldn't answer him. She simply fluttered close and held him, then waited in the world. It took the boy a long time, for he was now covered with the bark of a man, but he wanted to be held, and so, uprooting himself, he left the shade of his own heart and began to live.

- *While breathing deeply, consider the ways you prepare yourself to be loved.*

- *With each inbreath, lift up your prerequisites to being held.*

○ *With each outbreath, let go of all that is unnecessary.*

○ *Breathe slowly, and begin by allowing yourself to be held by the very air.*

The Ground We Walk

Walker, there is no path,
you make the path as you walk.

—ANTONIO MACHADO

I listened carefully as he described his little girl's first steps. He encouraged her to keep her eyes on him, and only when she didn't, did she stumble. Only when she lost her focus, when she became too conscious of the steps she was taking, did she fall.

I was afraid he was going to declare some parental primacy, that without his loving presence, his little girl wouldn't be able to make her way. But to my surprise, he understood her first steps more deeply as a wisdom that affects us all.

He stared off, offering slowly, "She made me realize that when I stop looking for a sense of truth, I stumble. When I lose my focus on what really matters, I fall."

This small story has stayed with me. For aren't we forever taking first steps, again and again? Don't we uncover a mystery of strength by looking out before us and bringing into focus a deeper sense of truth? Isn't balance, in reality, the ability to step quite naturally, like this little girl, without too much thought into everything larger than our fear?

○ *Sit quietly, and imagine one aspect of yourself as you would like to be: more loving, less afraid; more confident, less distrusting; more understanding, less critical.*

○ *Breathe evenly, and without troubling yourself with how, step with your heart into the field of this growth.*

In Our Own Element

A fish cannot drown in water.
A bird does not fall in air.
Each creature God made
must live in its own true nature.

—MECHTHILD OF MAGDEBURG

Somewhere in the Middle Ages in a remote part of Germany, this introspective seer came upon the wisdom that living in our own natural element is the surest way to know the inner prosperity of health, peace, and joy.

Her examples are striking; all we have to do is put the fish in air and the bird in water to see the dangers of being what we are not. Of course, it is very clear and obvious for both the fish and the bird where they belong. Not so for us humans.

Part of the blessing and challenge of being human is that we must discover our own true God-given nature. This is not some noble, abstract quest, but an inner necessity. For only by living in our own element can we thrive without anxiety. And since human beings are the only life form that can drown and still go to work, the only species that can fall from the sky and still fold laundry, it is imperative that we find that vital element that brings us alive.

I vividly recall my struggles as a teenager when my mother wanted me to be a lawyer and my father wanted me to be an architect. Somehow I knew I needed to be a poet; something in it brought me alive. The only one to understand was my boyhood friend Vic, who in the midst of qualifying strongly for pre-med studies realized he needed to be a florist. For something in working with flowers brought him alive. This is not about being a poet or a florist or a doctor or a lawyer or an architect. It is about the true vitality that waits beneath all occupations for us to tap into, if we can discover what we love. If you feel energy and excitement and a sense that life is happening for the first time, you are probably near your God-given nature. Joy in what we do is not an added feature; it is a sign of deep health.

○ *Sit quietly, and inhale your God-given nature. It is as near to you as air is to a bird.*

○ *Inhale and meditate on what you must be involved in to feel your own true nature.*

○ *Regardless of the job you're in,
how can you be more completely
who you are in a daily way?*

○ *As you move through your day,
involve yourself in one gesture of
vitality that puts you in touch with
your own true nature.*

Nicodemus and the Truth

How can one be born again?

—NICODEMUS TO JESUS

I often think of Nicodemus, the one Pharisee who secretly believed in Jesus and who would meet with him anonymously at night to have deep spiritual conversations, but who would never acknowledge his questions of spirit or his association with Jesus in the light of day. Of course, this did nothing to the essence of Jesus, but traumatically thwarted and plagued Nicodemus for the rest of his days.

This story shows us the quiet pain that comes from not honoring what we know to be true, even if all we know to be true are the questions we are asking. It is even more useful to realize that we each carry a Jesus and a Nicodemus within us; that is, we each have a divine inner voice that opens us to truth and a mediating social voice that is reluctant to show its truth to others.

The famous British child psychologist D. W. Winnicott called these aspects of personality our True Self and False Self. It is the True Self that lets us know what is authentic and what has become artificial, while the False Self is a diplomat of distrust, enforcing a lifestyle of guardedness, secrecy, and complaint.

In everyday terms, this means that each time we experience a change in reality as we know it, we must choose whether to declare or hide what we know to be true. At such moments, we either need to bring the way we have been living into accord with that shift of reality, or we need to resist the change. Thus, in daily ways, whether we live in our True or False Self depends on our willingness to stay real. And so, over time, staying real becomes the work of keeping our actions in the world connected to the truth of our inner being, allowing our True Self to see the light of day.

Very often, we continue, out of habit or fear, to behave in old ways, even though we know that the way of things has changed. Time and again, I have found myself at this crucial juncture: having to admit that what was essential is no longer essential and then needing to summon the courage to make the act of living essential again.

I know that every time I hear or see the truth but hold to the old way—of being or thinking or relating—I am giving my life over to the Nicodemus in me. And in so doing, I embark on a divided life, in which I listen to the divine inner voice secretly at night, but deny it day after day.

But this moment of inner embarrassment, when we catch ourselves in the act of split living, is also the recurring chance for us to honor once again what we know to be true. For anyone, no matter how wounded or distressed, can in a moment of truth let the God within show itself out here in the world. However small or fleeting, this one repeatable act can restore our common and vital sense of being alive.

○ *Sit quietly and recall the last time you felt a moment of inner embarrassment—that is, the last time you realized what you were doing was no longer authentic, but you kept doing it anyway.*

○ *If you can, meditate on what made you keep doing what you knew to be untrue. What were you afraid would happen if you honored the truth as you felt it?*

○ *If a similar situation were to happen tomorrow, how might you act differently?*

○ *If you can, don't blame yourself for struggling like Nicodemus. Rather, comfort the Nicodemus in you that it is safe to honor what it knows in the light of day.*

The Spoked Wheel

What we reach for may be different,
but what makes us reach is the same.

Imagine that each of us is a spoke in an Infinite Wheel, and, though each spoke is essential in keeping the Wheel whole, no two spokes are the same. The rim of that Wheel is our living sense of community, family, and relationship, but the common hub where all the spokes join is the one center where all souls meet. So, as I move out into the world, I live out my uniqueness, but when I dare to look into my core, I come upon the one common center where all lives begin. In that center, we are one and the same. In this way, we live out the paradox of being both unique and the same. For mysteriously and powerfully, when I look deep enough into you, I find me, and when you dare to hear my fear in the recess of your heart, you recognize it as your secret that you thought no one else knew. And that unexpected wholeness that is more than each of us, but common to all—that moment of unity is the atom of God.

Not surprisingly, like most people, in the first half of my life, I worked very hard to understand and strengthen my uniqueness. I worked hard to secure my place at the rim of the Wheel and so defined and valued myself by how different I was from everyone else. But in the second half of my life, I have been humbly brought to the center of that Wheel, and now I marvel at the mysterious oneness of our spirit.

Through cancer and grief and disappointment and unexpected turns in career—through the very breakdown and rearrangement of the things I have loved—I have come to realize that, as water smoothes stone and enters sand, we become each other. How could I be so slow? What I've always thought set me apart binds me to others.

Never was this more clear to me than when I was sitting in a waiting room at Columbia Presbyterian Hospital in New York City, staring straight into this Hispanic woman's eyes, she into mine. In that moment, I began to accept that we all see the same wonder, all feel the same agony, though we all speak in a different voice. I know now that each being born, inconceivable as it seems, is another Adam or Eve.

○ *Sit with a trusted loved one and take turns:*

○ *Name one defining trait of who you are that distinguishes you from others.*

○ *Name one defining trait of who you are that you have in common with others.*

○ *Discuss how you cope with the loneliness of what makes you unique from others, and how you cope with the experience of what makes you the same as others.*

The Impulse to Love

If somebody were to cut me into a
thousand pieces, every piece of me
would say that it loves. . . .

—CHRIS LUBBE

The man who said this is a deeply
spiritual person who is a native of
South Africa. He like many others grew
up under apartheid. He told me that he
was taught by his ancestors not to stay
bitter or vengeful, for hate eats up the
heart, and with a damaged heart, life is
not possible.

In a way, we are each confronted with
the same dilemma that Chris faces: how

to feel the pain of living without denying it and without letting that pain define us. Ultimately, no matter the burden we are given—apartheid, cancer, abuse, depression, addiction—once whittled to the bone, we are faced with a never-ending choice: to become the wound or to heal.

Terrible things are hard enough to experience the first time. Beyond their second and third and fourth experience as trauma, their impact can easily make us become terrible if we do not keep our want to love alive. Perhaps the most difficult challenge of being wounded is not turning our deepest loving nature over to the life and way of the wound.

This touching statement by this South African man affirms that the nature of the human spirit is irrepressible. Just as a vine or shrub—no matter how often it is cut back—will keep growing to the light, the human heart—no matter how

often it is cut—can reassert its impulse
to love.

- ○ *Center yourself and bring to mind*
  someone you admire who is still
  loving despite the pain they've
  experienced.

- ○ *Breathe slowly and open your*
  heart to the wisdom of their being.

- ○ *Breathe deeply now, and let your*
  heart-breath wash over your own
  pain, the way that surf softens
  footprints in sand.

Burying and Planting

*The culmination of one love, one
dream, one self, is the anonymous
seed of the next.*

There is very little difference between
burying and planting. For often,
we need to put dead things to rest, so
that new life can grow. And further, the
thing put to rest—whether it be a loved
one, a dream, or a false way of seeing—
becomes the fertilizer for the life about
to form. As the well-used thing joins
with the earth, the old love fertilizes
the new; the broken dream fertilizes the
dream yet conceived; the painful way

of being that strapped us to the world fertilizes the freer inner stance about to unfold.

This is very helpful when considering the many forms of self we inhabit over a lifetime. One self carries us to the extent of its usefulness and dies. We are then forced to put that once beloved skin to rest, to join it with the ground of spirit from which it came, so it may fertilize the next skin of self that will carry us into tomorrow.

There is always grief for what is lost and always surprise at what is to be born. But much of our pain in living comes from wearing a dead and useless skin, refusing to put it to rest, or from burying such things with the intent of hiding them rather than relinquishing them.

For every new way of being, there is a failed attempt mulching beneath the tongue. For every sprig that breaks surface, there is an old stick stirring underground. For every moment of joy sprouting, there is a new moment of struggle taking root.

We live, embrace, and put to rest our dearest things, including how we see ourselves, so we can resurrect our lives anew.

○ *Try to identify one aspect of your way in the world that has outlived its usefulness—a way of thinking or feeling, of speaking or relating.*

○ *Try to understand why you are still wearing it.*

○ *On loose paper, journal what this outlived aspect is and why you are still wearing it.*

○ *Take the paper and symbolically bury it somewhere special, giving thanks for how this outlived way has helped you to this point in your path.*

○ *Be kind to the new space that burying this has opened in you.*

○ *Water it and keep it in the light.*

A Silent Teacher

Only when I stop collecting evidence
do the stones begin to speak.

I want to speak to something very dear and obvious that has taken me my whole life to truly learn. We have touched on it elsewhere. More than knowledge, which I believe in, it involves knowing.

I have always been a reader. The worlds opened by honest voices throughout the ages have saved me from confusion and loneliness, time and time again. I have also spent roughly forty of my forty-nine years in school either as a student or a teacher. Not by chance, however, the classroom has enlarged over time to the living of life itself, and the teaching has involved less and less instructing and more and more the asking of simple things the secret of their simplicity.

But what I really want to say is that, astonishingly, the reward for truth, after all this way, is not justice or knowledge or expertise—though these things may happen—but joy; and the reward for kindness is not goodness or being thought well of or even having kindness returned—though these things may happen too. No, the reward for kindness, as well, is joy.

After the hard years of getting a doctorate, after studying on my own hundreds of sacred texts from so many different paths, I have learned that the blessing for experiencing oneness is not the strength or clarity that arrives with it, but, more deeply, a peace from dividedness.

Whether resting in a hospital bed when the pain has stopped, or waking in my lover's arms as her fingers ease the worry from my head, or falling asleep with the words of someone long dead lying open on my lap, the bareness of truth and compassion is the same. It returns me to a simple if rare moment in which thinking and feeling and knowing and being are all the same. It is this enlivening moment—so hard to find and so elusive to hold—that is my silent teacher.

○ *Close your eyes, and bring into focus one thing you know from reading or studying that has helped you. Note where it comes into your awareness. Does it come*

alive in your head, in your heart,
or in your stomach?

○ *Bring into focus one important*
  thing you have learned from liv-
  ing. Note where it comes into your
  awareness. Where does it come
  alive?

○ *Without judging either, note the*
  sameness or difference in how
  these knowings live in you.

WEEK 17

All That We Are Not

Discernment is a process of letting go
of what we are not.

—FATHER THOMAS KEATING

I can easily over-identify with my emo-
tions and roles, becoming what I feel:
I am angry. . . . I am divorced. . . . I am
depressed. . . . I am a failure. . . . I am
nothing but my confusion and my sadness. . . .

No matter how we feel in any one
moment, we are not just our feelings,
our roles, our traumas, our prescription
of values, or our obligations or ambi-
tions. It is so easy to define ourselves by

the moment of struggle we are wrestling with. It is a very human way, to be consumed by what moves through us.

In contrast, I often think of how Michelangelo sculpted, how he saw the sculpture waiting, already complete, in the uncut stone. He would often say that his job was to carve away the excess, freeing the thing of beauty just waiting to be released.

It helps me to think of spiritual discernment in this way. Facing ourselves, uncovering the meaning in our hard experiences, the entire work of consciousness speaks to a process by which we sculpt away the excess, all that we are not, finding and releasing the gesture of soul that is already waiting, complete, within us. Self-actualization is this process applied to our life on Earth. The many ways we suffer, both inwardly and outwardly, are the chisels of God freeing

the thing of beauty that we have carried
within since birth.

- *Sit quietly, and as you breathe, feel
  all that troubles you rise through
  your body.*

- *As you breathe, allow these troubles to move away from you.*

- *Breathe deeply and accept the still-
  ness that comes. It is the skin of
  your soul, waiting in its complete-
  ness for you to carve away the
  excess of your very human moods.*

WEEK 18

Not Two

To reach Accord,
just say, "Not Two!"
—SENG-TS'AN

Almost fourteen hundred years ago, one of the first Chinese sages we know of offered this brief retort to those who pestered him for advice—"Not Two!"

This reply is as pertinent as it is mysterious. To make sense of it, we need to understand what isn't said: that everything that divides and separates removes us from what is sacred, and so weakens our chances for joy.

How can this be? Well, to understand this, we must open ourselves to an even deeper truth: that everything—you and I and the people we mistrust and even the things we fear—everything at heart follows the same beat of life pulsing beneath all the distractions and preferences we can create.

Once divided from the common beat of life, we are cut off from the abundance and strength of life, the way an organ cut out of the body dies. So, to find peace, to live peace, we need to keep restoring our original Oneness. We need to experience that ancient and central beat which we share with everything that exists. In feeling this common beat, we begin to swell again with the common strength of everything alive.

Yet we tend to lose our way when faced with choices. Tension builds around decisions because we quickly sort and name one way as good and another as bad. This quickly twists into an either/or sense that one way is right and another is wrong. In prizing what we prefer, we start to feel a thirst for something particular, which getting we call "success," and a fear of not getting it, which we then call "failure." From all this, we begin to feel the tightening pressure not to make a terrible mistake. Thus, we are often stymied and confused because we forget that—beneath our sorting of everything into good and bad, right and wrong, success and failure—all the choices still hold the truth and strength of life, no matter what we prefer.

To be certain, sharing a common beat does not mean that everything is the same, for things are infinite in how they differ. And faced with the richness of life, we can't value everything the same. But when we believe that only what we want holds the gold, then we find ourselves easily depressed by what we lack. Then we are pained by what we perceive as the difference between here and there, between what we have and what we need.

We still need to discern the ten thousand things we meet, but holding them to the light of our heart, we can say, "Not Two! Only One!" and realize there are no wrong turns, only unexpected paths.

○ *Meditate on a choice that is before you.*

○ *Identify the distinct options you have.*

○ *Try not to view these options with the urgency of what you prefer; rather focus on the experience each option might offer you.*

○ *Try not to attach your sense of identity to any one option.*

○ *If you don't get what you want, try not to see it as a failure but as an unexpected opening.*

Moments, Not Words

Like the moon,
come out from behind the clouds!
And Shine!

— BUDDHA

When I think of those who've taught me how to love, moments come to mind, not words. As far back as grade school, when Lorrie wouldn't stop spinning when recess ended. Spinning to a deeper, higher call, she laughed, her little head back, her arms wide, trying to hug the world.

Then, the day Kennedy was shot, there was my choir teacher, Mr. P., crying for a man he didn't know, letting us go home, but I came back to hear him play a sad piano to what he thought was an empty room. And Grandma holding my little hands open on her basement steps, saying, "These are the oldest things you own."

Or the changing faces I would wake to at the foot of my bed while recovering from surgery. Or my father-in-law watering black walnuts six inches high that wouldn't be fully grown for a hundred and fifty years. Or my oldest friend who always listens like a lake.

Though words can carry love, they often point to it. It is the picking up of something that has dropped, and the giving of space for someone to discover for themselves what it means to be human, and the forgiving of mistakes when we realize what we've done.

- ○ *Center yourself and bring to mind three people who have taught you how to love.*

- ○ *As you breathe, recall the moment that revealed each lesson.*

- ○ *Discuss these teachings with a loved one.*

WEEK 20

What Your Life Asks of You

How are you tending
to the emerging story of your life?

—CAROL HEGEDUS

Like many of us, I seem to be continually challenged not to hide who
I am. Over and over, I keep finding
myself in situations that require me to
be all of who I am in order to make my
way through.

Whether breaking a pattern of imbal-
ance with a lifelong friend, or admitting
my impatience to listen to my lover, or

owning my envy of a colleague, or even confronting the self-centeredness of strangers stealing parking spaces, I find I must be present—even if I say nothing. I find I must not suppress my full nature, or my life doesn't emerge.

Aside from the feeling of integrity or satisfaction that comes over me when I can fully be myself, I am finding that being who I am—not hiding any of myself—is a necessary threshold that I must meet or my life will not evolve. It is a doorway I must make my way to or nothing happens. My life just stalls.

Tending our stories means that our lies must open if we are to live in the mystery; our ways of hiding, no matter how subtle, must relax open if we are to be.

○ *Center yourself and meditate on the emerging story of your life.*

○ *Breathe slowly and consider what your life asks of you so that it can emerge.*

○ *Breathe fully and consider how you can better meet this inner requirement.*

In the Ocean of Spirit

Though the wind enlivens the tree,
the tree is not the wind.
And though life enlivens us,
we are not the Source.

Everywhere we are given examples of
how the life-giving elements move
through us and bring us to life. Consider
how fish make up the sea, in fact depend
on the sea, and yet the sea, though found
in each fish, cannot be contained in any
one fish. Consider how the tree has no
control over the movement of the wind,
any more than the fish has control of the
movement of the sea.

Humbly, this gives us a way to understand the vast life of spirit. For like the tree and the fish, we as human beings have no control over the movement of grace. Souls, like fish, make up the ocean of all spirit, depending on that element, and yet the ocean of grace, though found in each soul, cannot be contained in any one soul.

If we understand this, it affects the way we live. For no matter your spiritual lens or the names you prefer for the mystery, human beings make up the world of God, depend on the world of God, and yet the world of God, though found in each being, cannot be contained in any one life.

When we refuse this truth, we begin to self-destruct, because in our pride and will we try to contain and control more than any one human being can. Only when we recognize the elemental relationship of soul to spirit—of individual life to the stream of life—only then do we paradoxically have the blessing and energy of all life.

If I am honest in looking at all my attempts to love and be loved, I must admit that this also holds true in matters of the heart. For aren't all our passions and yearnings little fish that make up a greater sea of Love? Don't we depend on the Love that surrounds us to bring us alive within? And yet the ocean of Love, though found in each heart, cannot be contained in any one heart. In truth, the essence of Love, as Jesus affirms, is greater than all the hearts that claim to have it.

But how does knowing all this help us live? For myself, I can only offer that I often feel like a tree standing up to wind. And just as we can only hear a great wind for the trees that stand against it, we can only know God by leaning our soul into the wind of our experience.

- *Watch the wind move through a familiar tree.*

- *Watch until the wind has left, and notice how even when still the branches sway slightly.*

- *Notice how even what seems like still air is just a subtle wind.*

- *Meditate on how similar the life of spirit is as it moves through us.*

- *Feel the force of life like a subtle wind move through you as you breathe.*

Our Ability to Try

> If you try to teach before you learn
> or leave before you stay,
> you will lose your ability to try.

There are so many ways we can divorce ourselves from our own experience. I can remember, as a young man fearing the pain of being hurt by love, I became endlessly involved in advising others in their struggles with love. I can remember, when fearing the sadness and pain of conflict with dear ones, leaving notes rather than facing them in person, trying to leap over the need to go through the real stuff face to face. I can remember, when facing the next horrific chemo treatment, trying to anticipate and prepare endlessly for every possible instant of pain and fear, only to discover that no amount of preparation can keep me from my experience.

Each of these separations—teaching before learning, leaving before staying, anticipating rather than entering—left me drained of my deepest resource, the energy of my life force. Removing myself, even from pain, only left me pale and unable to continue.

When needle or hand or rain or sun hits the skin, the only thing to do is meet its exact touch from the inside. For this moment of inner meeting outer releases an electricity of spirit that gifts us with a tenderness for being awake.

○ *Sit with a trusted loved one, and after centering yourselves, take turns:*

○ *Let your loved one slowly place their palm on your heart.*

○ *As their hand reaches and lands on your heart, practice meeting its touch with the energy of your inwardness.*

Two Heart Cells Beating

> If you place two living heart cells from
> different people in a Petrie dish, they
> will in time find and maintain a third
> and common beat.
> —MOLLY VASS

This biological fact holds the secret of all relationship. It is cellular proof that beneath any resistance we might pose and beyond all our attempts that fall short, there is in the very nature of life itself some essential joining force. This inborn ability to find and enliven a common beat is the miracle of love.

This force is what makes compassion possible, even probable. For if two cells can find the common pulse beneath everything, how much more can full hearts feel when all excuses fall away?

This drive toward a common beat is the force beneath curiosity and passion. It is what makes strangers talk to strangers, despite the discomfort. It is how we risk new knowledge. For being still enough, long enough, next to anything living, we find a way to sing the one voiceless song.

Yet we often tire ourselves by fighting how our hearts want to join, seldom realizing that both strength and peace come from our hearts beating in unison with all that is alive. It feels incredibly uplifting that without even knowing each other, there exists a common beat between all hearts, just waiting to be felt.

It brings to mind the time that the great poet Pablo Neruda, near the end of his life, stopped while traveling at the Lota coal mine in rural Chile. He stood there stunned, as a miner, rough and blackened by his work inside the earth, strode straight for Neruda, embraced him, and said, "I have known you a long time, my brother."

Perhaps this is the secret—that every time we dare to voice what beats within, we invite some other cell of heart to find what lives between us and sing.

○ *Breathe deeply in silence and feel the beat of your heart.*

○ *Meditate on the common beat the cells of your heart carry.*

○ *Let this beat sound like a beacon from you.*

○ *As you enter your day, keep sending the beat of your heart to*

*everything around you. Do this
with your regular breathing.*

○ *Be aware of the moments you feel
energized or filled with emotion. It
is in the life of these moments that
you are in full relationship with the
world.*

Growing Inside the Song

What lies behind us
and what lies before us
are tiny matters
compared to
what lies within us.

—RALPH WALDO EMERSON

I saw a woman singing while pregnant and imagined how the rhythms of song affected the life forming within her, imagined the song drawing her unborn child's soul closer to its time in the world, the way light works on a root strengthening underground.

I watched her sing and realized that the life within her was growing inside the song. I looked around the room, for we were in a circle of song, and everyone's singing was bringing their soul closer to its time in the world. The nervous man was less nervous while singing, and the insecure woman next to me was relaxing her unworthiness as she sang, and I was able to drop my replaying of wounds while my mouth was open and my eyes were closed.

It was then I realized that regardless of the words or the melody, this effort to sing is a way to open the passageways between what is growing within and what is growing without.

I now believe it is important that we sing while pregnant with our dreams and troubles and want of truth and love. Important that we attend our little seed of spirit with the same care we would offer an unborn life forming within us.

Essential that we care for our unique body as a carrier of life magically forming within us as we make it through our days.

- *Center yourself and meditate with your hands on your belly, imagining that you are pregnant with a form of yourself growing within you.*

- *Breathe deeply, and when comfortable, give voice to your breath, letting your breathing have whatever sound it will.*

- *Breathe slowly and fully, knowing this simple voiced breath is a song.*

- *Breathe-sing while your hands hold your spirit forming within you.*

Honey of My Failures

Last night, as I was sleeping,
I dreamt—marvelous error!—
that I had a beehive
here inside my heart.
And the golden bees
were making white combs
and sweet honey
from my old failures.

—ANTONIO MACHADO

It seems impossible, but every humbled life has cried it is so: The sweetness of living comes to us when the very humanness we regret and try to hide, our seeming flaws and shameful secrets, are worked by time and nature into a honey all their own. Ultimately, it is where we are not perfect—where we are broken and cracked, where the wind whistles through—that is the stuff of transformation.

Like other people, many of the things I've wanted to be have crumbled over time into cinders that have sparked the very next dream. And the hurtful things I've never meant to say have thickened my tongue over time into a kindness I didn't think possible. And each time I've failed at being what someone else needed or wanted or hoped for, each time I've failed at being what I needed or wanted or hoped for—each failure at love has solidified into unexpected learnings. The painful shavings of one love have become the spices of joy in the next.

They say that Cupid's shafts, when not landing in the heart, were ordinary arrows that wounded the innocent. Like

Cupid, we try so hard, but missing, hurt those along the way until we land squarely in the heart. And, when we miss, we are wounded as much as those we wound.

None of this lessens the pain of our journey, but it gives me comfort that our failures—our unexpected stumblings—are the very human paste from which we are made sweet.

Just know, when everything is falling apart, that you are preparing the ground of you for something ripe that can't yet be seen, but which, in time, will be tasted.

○ *Sit quietly with a trusted friend and meditate on one relationship you believe you failed at.*

○ *After a period of silence, discuss how you think you failed.*

○ *Discuss how you carry this fail-ure, how it affects your current relationships.*

○ *Identify, if you can, one way you have softened and grown in your heart for having experienced this failure.*

○ *Though the relationship didn't last, bear witness to one sweetness that lingers from it.*

The Gift of Prayer

Prayer is not asking. It is a longing of the soul. It is daily admission of one's weakness. . . . And so, it is better in prayer to have a heart without words than words without a heart.

—GANDHI

This great spiritual teacher reminds us that prayer of the deepest kind is more a pledge of gratitude for what has already been received than a request or plea for something not yet experienced. Such an effort refreshes the soul.

Implicit in Gandhi's instruction is the need to surrender to our lives here on

Earth. By admitting our weaknesses, we lay down all the masks we show the world and as we do so, what is holy floods in.

I once saw a blind man rocking endlessly in the sun, an unstoppable smile on his face. Not a word was uttered. To me, he was a priest, a shaman, and his whole being was praying and shouting in silence that the day, beyond his blindness, was happily enough.

This is what the heart knows beyond all words, if we can find a way to listen: that beyond our small sense of things a magnificent light surrounds us, more than anyone could ask for. This is what prayer as gratitude can open us to.

○ *Center yourself, and as you breathe, close your eyes and cease all asking.*

○ *Simply breathe with gratitude for the air.*

○ *Relax and feel your frailties and imperfections, and let the simple air fill them.*

○ *Breathe deeply and slowly, and from your tender imperfect insides, ask for nothing and give nothing; just feel without words for your soul's place in the fabric of things.*

Practicing

As a man in his last breath
drops all he is carrying
each breath is a little death
that can set us free.

Breathing is the fundamental unit of risk, the atom of inner courage that leads us into authentic living. With each breath, we practice opening, taking in, and releasing. Literally, the teacher is under our nose. When anxious, we simply have to remember to breathe.

So often we make a commitment to change our ways, but stall in the face of old reflexes as new situations arise. When gripped by fear or anxiety, the reflex is to hold on, speed up, or remove oneself. Yet when we feel the reflex to hold on, that is usually the moment we need to let go. When we feel the urgency to speed up, that is typically the instant we need to slow down. Often when we feel the impulse to flee, it is the opportunity to face ourselves. Taking a deep meditative breath, precisely at this moment, can often break the momentum of anxiety and put our psyche in neutral. From here, we just might be able to step in another direction.

I'm not talking about external moments of anxiety here, but inner moments of truth. Certainly, when an accident is unfolding, we need to get out of the way; when a loved one falls, we need to try to hold them. Rather, I'm talking about fear of love and truth and God, fear of change and the unknown. I'm talking about how we all grip tightly to what we know, even if we hurt ourselves in the process.

Dropping all we carry—all our preconceptions, our interior lists of the ways we've failed and the ways we've been wronged, all the secret burdens we work at maintaining—dropping all regret and expectation lets our mentality die. Dropping all we have constructed as imperative allows us to be born again into the simplicity of spirit that arises from unencumbered being.

It is often overwhelming to imagine changing our entire way of life. Where do we begin? How do we take down a wall that took twenty-five or fifty years to erect? Breath by breath. Little death by little death. Dropping all we carry instant by instant. Trusting that what has done the carrying, if freed, will carry us.

○ *Sit by yourself, alone, in a safe place, and think of the last situation that made you anxious.*

○ *Ask yourself: What specifically made you uncomfortable? In tensing, what did you cling to in your mind?*

○ *Place both your discomfort and your clinging before you now.*

○ *In this safe place, touch what scared you. It can't hurt you now.*

○ *In this safe place, drop what your mind clung to. It can't help you now.*

○ *Repeat this several times while breathing slowly and deeply.*

○ *Breathe. Feel in detail what rises in you without the discomfort or the clinging.*

○ *Breathe. This is the God in you. Bow to it.*

WEEK 28

The One Direction

Live deep enough
and there is only one direction.

No matter whom the apprentice talked to, if she listened close enough and long enough, the words all went back to the same source, as if there were only one large thing speaking. No matter how many eyes she looked deeply into, they all eventually revealed the same shimmer, as if there were only one large thing seeing. No matter how many pains she soothed, the cries all sounded from the same human hurt, as if there were only one large thing feeling.

When she brought all this to her master, her master walked her in silence through the woods to a clearing, where they sat on a fallen tree. The light was flooding through, covering everything. The master placed a stone in her one hand and a small flower in her other hand, and said, "Feel the warmth from both stone and flower. See how both are covered differently with the same light. Now trace the light of each back to the sun."

The apprentice heard the one large thing speaking in the master's voice, saw the one large thing shimmer in the master's eyes, and even felt the same human hurt in the master's soft silence. The light grew even stronger and the master said, "We are all just small stones and little flowers searching for our sun. What you have seen under words, behind many eyes, and beneath all cries is the one direction."

○ Meditate on one recent moment of lightheartedness you have felt. Breathe deeply and smile.

○ Now meditate on one recent moment of lightheartedness you witnessed in a loved one or friend. Breathe deeply and smile.

○ Continue your deep breathing, and let these two moments find their sameness.

○ Focus on this lightness of heart as you would a sun out of view, and feel the one direction.

Opening Our Deepest Eyes

> The inner life of any great thing will be incomprehensible to me until I develop and deepen an inner life of my own.
>
> —PARKER J. PALMER

Everyone has an inner life; it's just a matter of opening it. What Parker Palmer wisely suggests is that we can only feel something to the degree that we are willing to meet its depth. Just as we must open our eyes—must raise our lids—to see, we must raise our barriers and open our hearts and minds, if we are to see and feel the essence of the life around us.

To develop our own inner life is tantamount to opening our deepest eyes. It has much to do with raising our walls, with living from our own depths so we can experience the depths around us.

Too often, while cut off from our inwardness, we complain that the things about us are shallow and boring, not worth our attention, when, more often than not, it is we who are out of touch.

To see deeply, we must open deeply.

○ *Bring to mind something or someone you've dismissed, and bring it or this person before your heart's opened eye.*

○ *Surround the image with your deepest breathing.*

○ *After a time, ask yourself, Does this thing or person seem any different?*

More Than Our Mistakes

> The buffalo fed on the buffalo grass that
> was fertilized by their own droppings.
> This grass had deep roots bound to the
> earth and was resistant to drought.
> —DAVID PEAT

Try as we will, we cannot escape the making of mistakes. But fortunately, the ever-humbling cycle of growing strong roots comes from eating what grows from our own shit, from digesting and processing our own humanity. Like the buffalo, we are nourished by what sprouts from our own broken trail. What we trample and leave behind fertilizes what will feed us. No one is exempt.

A pipe falls on a dancer's leg and the dancer must reinvent herself, while the worker who dropped it is driven to volunteer with crippled veterans. A dear friend discovers small bulbous tumors and his tulips begin to speak, and when he dies, his nurse begins a garden. Things come apart and join sometimes faster than we can cope. But we evolve in spite of our limitations, and though we break and make mistakes, we are always mysteriously more than what is broken. Indeed, we somehow grow from the soil of our mistakes. And often in the process, the things we refuse to let go of are somehow forced from our grip.

I have been broken and have failed so many times that my sense of identity has sprouted and peeled like an onion. But because of this, I have lived more than my share of lives and feel both young and old at once, with a sudden heart that cries just to meet the air. Now, on the other side of all I've suffered so far, everything, from the quick song of birds to the peace trapped inside a fresh brook's gurgle, is rare and uncertain. Now I want to stand naked before every wind; and though I'm still frightened I will break, I somehow know it's all a part—even the fright—of the rhythm of being alive.

You see, no one ever told me that as snakes shed skin, as trees snap bark, the human heart peels, crying when forced open, singing when loved open. Now I understand that whatever keeps us from burning truth as food, whatever tricks the heart into thinking we can hide in the open, whatever makes us look everywhere but in the core, this is the smoke that drives us from what is living. And whatever keeps us coming back, coming up, whatever makes us build a home out of straw, out of heartache, out of nothing, whatever ignites us to see again for the very first time, this is the bluish flame that keeps the Earth grinding to the sun.

○ *Light a candle. Sit quietly and focus on the blue part of the flame as you meditate on one loss you carry within you. It could be a person who has died or left your life. Or a dream that has evaporated.*

○ *Sift through the feelings that surround this loss and find one detail that seems worth saving. It might be represented by a pen or book that someone used. Or a favorite chair. Or a piece of music. Or a gardening tool.*

○ *Holding this detail in your heart, look into the bluish flame and meditate on the gift you carry from what is gone.*

○ *Now use this detail, if you can, to help you build what is presently before you.*

○ *Try to infuse what is worth saving from what you've lost.*

○ *Use the old to build the new.*

Grace Comes to the Wave

Enlightenment for a wave is the moment
the wave realizes that it is water. At that
moment, all fear of death disappears.

—THICH NHAT HANH

Much like the life of ordinary waves, we as human beings are gathered in our passion out of a larger home, that sea of infinite spirit, and propelled from an unfathomable depth, we mount and curl and crest and spray, only to subside back into that from which we come.

Profoundly, grace comes to the wave when it realizes what it is made of. Since it has risen from the very same water into which it will crash, its fear of ending is somehow lessened. For it is already a part of where it is going. Can it be that you and I, like simple waves, experience such an enlightenment the instant we realize that we are all made of the same water? Can truly knowing this, the way that waves know wind, lessen our fear of death?

I think I experienced something like this while healing from my rib surgery. I was broken of all difference, dashed of all the ways I could distinguish myself from others. In this tired and dizzied state, I could see that we are all made of the same stuff and that life before me and after me is probably no different than the lights and shadows flickering off my cells right now. Like the wave, aware that it is water, I realized briefly that my skin is a very thin boundary and that wherever I am going is the same as where I am. As a human being now aware of this larger sea of spirit, my fear of death has lessened, though, even as I write this, I don't want to die.

I think now that the other way to read all this is to say that enlightenment is the moment we realize that we are made of love. At that moment, all fear of living disappears. For grace comes to the heart when it realizes what it is made of and what it has risen from. In that moment, grace comforts us, that no matter the joy or pain along the way, we are already a part of where we are going. Enlightenment for a heart on Earth is the moment we accept that it is the loving that makes waves of us all, again and again and again.

○ *Breathe slowly, and meditate on the nearest window. Note how the same air gathers outside the window and inside the window.*

○ *Breathe slowly, and meditate on how your mouth is like that window. Note how the same air gathers outside of you as well as inside of you.*

○ *Breathe deeply, and feel the essence of everything move in and out of the window that is you.*

Wu Feng

In the end, it is not enough to think what we know. We must live it. For only by living it can Love show itself as the greatest principle.

The way that heat allows ice to thaw and irrigate the earth, so our capacity to embody what we know—our quiet need to bring what lives within into accord with how we meet the days—this ancient act of integrity allows Love to show itself as the deepest sort of gravity.

There was a quiet man whose life-changing moment of such courage is inspiring. He was Wu Feng, a Manchurian diplomat of the 1700s who was posted with an aboriginal tribe in the outskirts of Taiwan. Wu Feng befriended the aboriginal chief, whose tribe beheaded one of its members every year as a form of sacrifice.

Each year Wu Feng pleaded with all of his compassion and reverence for life that the chief put an end to this custom. The chief would listen respectfully as Wu Feng would plead, and then after listening and bowing, the chief would summon the chosen tribe member and without hesitation behead him.

Finally, after living with the tribe for twenty-five years, Wu Feng once more pleaded with the chief to stop this senseless killing. But this time, when the tribe member was called forth, Wu Feng took his place and said, "If you will kill this time, it will be me."

The chief stared long into his friend's eyes, and having grown to love Wu

Feng, he could not kill him. From that day, the practice of beheading stopped.

Of course, Wu Feng could have been killed, but his courage shows us that at a certain point, how we live inside takes priority. At a certain point for each of us, talk evaporates and words cannot bring Love into the open. Only the soul's presence coming from us can attract the soul's presence in others.

○ *As you breathe, be honest with yourself; that is, see things in your life as they are.*

○ *Is there a situation in your life in which a part of you is being sacrificed like the member of the aboriginal tribe?*

○ *Are you repeatedly being asked to deny who you are in some relationship?*

- *If so, can the Wu Feng in you stop talking and make itself present?*

- *If the answer is yes, simply honor that such a spirit of embodiment lives within you.*

- *Simply ask the question today. Trust your spirit to know when and how to do so.*

In the Likeness of Everything

Everything in the Universe is inter-
connected. Within each it is reflected.
—LOURDES PITA

I think this insight explains why we
are so drawn to certain things: why,
of all the fallen branches, I will go to
the one that most resembles the way
I've had to bend all my life; why, of
all the places you could return to, you
choose the lip of a cliff worn feature-
less by wind, because it lets you feel the

worn lip of your heart that you show no one.

It seems that we humans have always been drawn to find ourselves in the life about us. But too often, in doing so we break everything down until everything resembles us. Too often, though we seldom mean to, we take in life the way we do food, chewing it into unrecognizable bits that need to be swallowed. But the kind of food that living offers must be taken in whole, as it is, or it loses its wisdom and power and grace.

So, this is our ongoing challenge: not to turn everything into us. In truth, the deepest function of humility is that it helps us take experience in on its own terms, not violating its own nature—all in an effort to be nourished by life that is different from us. Through this effort, we find the corresponding seeds of such life in us. They are the common seeds of grace that can sustain us.

In truth, we each carry within our own innate makeup, like chromosomes, the minute aspects of everything that forms the Universe. And so, the art of freedom becomes the necessary adventure of grasping the secrets that are everywhere in the open and stirring their aspects within us, in such a way that we come alive: learning from the fish how to surface and dive, from the flower how to open and accept, from the stone how to crack and let light in, and from the birds that wings are more useful at times than brains.

Rather than finding ourselves in everything, we are challenged daily to find everything in ourselves, till being human is evolving inwardly in the likeness of everything, shaping ourselves to the wonders we find, until like birds, who have known this forever, we too make song at the mere appearance of light.

- ○ *Sit quietly and bring to mind a favorite place in nature where you like to go. It might be an open field, or a waterfall, or a stream, or a path in the woods.*

- ○ *Go there in your mind and feel the one aspect that keeps bringing you back there. It might be the wind through the grass, or the sound of the water, or the light through colored leaves.*

- ○ *In your mind, enlarge the one compelling aspect and enter it more fully. Become the grass or the water or the leaf.*

○ *Breathe slowly and let what you love about this place teach you how you are grasslike or waterlike or leaflike.*

Meeting the World

You must meet the outer world with your
inner world or existence will crush you.

There is a wind that keeps blowing
since the beginning of time, and in
every language ever spoken, it continues to whisper, You must meet the outer
world with your inner world or existence will crush you. If inner does not
meet outer, our lives will collapse and
vanish. Though we often think that hiding our inwardness will somehow pro-
tect or save us, it is quite the opposite.
The heart is very much like a miraculous

balloon. Its lightness comes from staying full. Meeting the days with our heart prevents collapse.

This is why ninety-year-old widows remain committed to tending small flowers in spring; why ten-year-olds with very little to eat care for stray kittens, holding them to their skinny chests; why painters going blind paint more; why composers going deaf write great symphonies. This is why when we think we can't possibly try again, we let out a sigh that goes back through the centuries, and then, despite all our experience, we inhale and try again.

○ *Center yourself and breathe slowly and deeply.*

○ *As you breathe, feel your lungs fill and empty like a balloon.*

○ *As you breathe, realize that your heart is filling and emptying itself of an inner air.*

○ *During your day, let this inner air meet the world whenever you feel overwhelmed.*

Surfacing Through

This night will pass . . .
Then we have work to do . . .
Everything has to do
with loving and not loving. . . .

—RUMI

Very often, when hurt or depressed
or anxious, we encounter powerful
feelings like ghosts without a body, trying to pour themselves into us, trying to
dominate our lives. They seem to gather
in the cave of our pain, stoking our
wounds like stones in a fire that keeps
them warm.

After years of struggling to let my painful feelings out, I'm learning that the other side of this, which is just as essential to my well-being, is not to let the hurt or depression or anxiety set up camp inside me.

I must confess it has taken me all this way to fully understand that the purpose of surfacing these powerful feelings is to continually empty my heart and mind of its sediment, so that new life can make its way into me.

There are dangers to not letting such feelings out. But once felt, there are dangers as well to not letting such feelings move on through. For just as our lungs must stay clear for the next mouthful of air, our heart must stay unobstructed for the next feeling we encounter.

There is no freedom until we dance the ghosts from the chambers of our wounds, until we pile our wounds like stones at the mouth of our own quarries.

○ Center yourself and call into view a painful feeling that has stayed with you too long.

○ Through your meditation, enter a dialogue with this feeling and ask why it will not go; just what does it need in order to leave?

○ Breathe steadily and live with what it says.

The Kinship of Gratitude

> When you make the two one, when you
> make the inner as outer and the outer as
> inner—then shall you enter the kingdom.
> —JESUS

The goal of all experience is to remove whatever might keep us from being whole. The things we learn through love and pain reduce our walls and bring our inner and outer life together, and all the while the friction of being alive erodes whatever impediments remain.

But the simplest and deepest way to make who we are at one with the world is through the kinship of gratitude.

Nothing brings the worlds of spirit and earth together more quickly.

To be grateful means giving thanks for more than just the things we want, but also for the things that surmount our pride and stubbornness. Sometimes the things I've wanted and worked for, if I actually received them, would have crushed me.

Sometimes just giving thanks for the mystery of it all brings everything and everyone closer, the way suction pulls streams of water together. So take a chance and openly give thanks, even if you're not sure what for, and feel the plenitude of all that is living brush up against your heart.

○ *Sit quietly and meditate on what keeps you from knowing yourself.*

○ *Breathe deeply, and lower your walls with an offering of gratitude that is not attached to any one thing.*

○ *Now inhale with gratitude and exhale what remains in the way.*

○ *Repeat this several times through-out your day.*

The Heart's Blossom

Courage is the heart's blossom.

All courage is threshold crossing. Often there is a choice: to enter the burning building or not, to speak the truth or not, to stand before oneself without illusion or not. But there is another sort of courage we are talking about here—the kind when afterward, the courageous are puzzled to be singled out as brave. They often say, I had no choice. I had to run in that building for that child. Or I had to quit my job or I would have died.

Despite all consequence, there is an inevitable honoring of what is true, and at this deep level of inner voice, it is not a summoning of will, but a following of true knowing.

My own life is a trail of such following. Time and again, I have heard deep callings that felt inevitable and which I could have ignored, but only at great risk of something essential perishing.

It was this honoring of what is true that guided me through my cancer experience: saying no to brain surgery and yes to rib surgery, saying yes to chemo and no to chemo. Each decision appeared both courageous and illogical to my doctors. Since then, I have been called heroic for surviving, which is like championing an eagle for finding its nest, and I have been condemned as selfish for seeking the Truth, which is like blaming a turtle for finding the deep.

Courage of this sort is the result of being authentic. It is available to all and its reward, far more than respect, is the opening of joy.

○ *Meditate on a decision that you are struggling with.*

○ *Rather than focusing on your fear of what might or might not happen, try opening to what feels true.*

○ *Without strategizing or imagining the consequences of honoring what feels true, simply let the truth as you know it rise within you.*

○ *As you move through your day, let what is true fill you, even if you don't quite understand it.*

One Drop of Truth at a Time

It is the fullness of our attention to whatever is near that has birds fly out of God's mouth.

The months relax and the ice enclosing a bent-over branch thaws, and the snow drops and the branch springs back up after its deathlike sleep. The tree coming into spring teaches us how to let go into renewal. For this is how the freeze around a broken heart thaws. In another part of the world, small brilliant fish mouth pebbles along the ocean sand, sucking off bits of food and spitting back the rest. This is how they comb the bottom, and these small limbless creatures teach us how to suffer and move on, how to sift through what is nourishing and how to give back the rest. And high in the mountains, away from the eyes of others, a small cave with its singular drip collects clear water that is the heartbeat of the mountain. So the center of the Earth itself shows us how to be: one drop of clearness at a time, collecting in the moist center that keeps the soul alive.

These are just a few examples of an essential relatedness that exists between all things. In practice, if we look closely with our whole being at anything—plants, trees, the human heart, emptiness, fish, even the worn gears of a watch—the same core of deep instruction will rise before us in a language that waits beneath words. The world, it seems, both natural and constructed, is an endless net of particular lessons, each made of the same compelling thread that is always hiding in the open, simply waiting for our complete attention to reveal itself. By pulling at these threads, I have discovered, again and again, the deep and common way of things that is embedded in everything.

So when confusion or pain seems to tighten what is possible, when sadness or frustration shrinks your sense of well-being, when worry or fear agitates the peace right out of you, try lending your attention to the nearest thing. Try watching how the dust lifts and resettles when you blow on it. Watch how the pawprints of your neighbor's retriever, if stared at long enough, turn into unexpected symbols. Watch how the one shell you brought back three years ago from the sea reveals itself, at last, as a

face that is telling you how to continue.
Give your full attention over to the nearest patch of life—to how an apple peels
and juices—and after a while each thing
attended will reveal yet another way
back to the center.

- ○ *This is a walking meditation.*
  Center yourself and breathe deeply
  as you slowly step into the world
  nearby.

- ○ *Once centered, look around and*
  focus on one thing that seems to
  have the rhythm of what you are
  feeling. It might be the slight sway
  of a bush or the tumble of a cup
  blowing down the street.

- ○ *Breathe slowly and give your*
  full attention to the small outer
  rhythm that is matching your
  mood.

○ *Breathe and watch until the rhythm you are seeing and the rhythm you are feeling reveal their common truth.*

Talking Fast

Live loud enough in your heart
and there is no need to speak.

There was a time in my life during my years in college when I was so talkative that the waterfall of words kept others at a safe distance. Of course, in time, this cascade pushed others away. But what I didn't realize till much later was that I kept talking faster and louder to the world around me because I couldn't hear the world within me. Of course, the more noise I made, the less chance I had of having what was real enter me or rise from me. It became a damning cycle. So often, we mistake the need to hear with the need to be heard. All that talk was a way of reaching out to others with my heart. Ultimately, it was all based on the fear that if I didn't throw my heart out there—through endless words and gestures and questions—I would be left alone. It's taken me many years to learn that the world comes flooding in if I can only keep myself open.

It remains important to reach out and to express oneself, but underneath that is the need to be porous and real. Through the opened heart, the world comes rushing in, the way oceans fill the smallest hole along the shore. It is the quietest sort of miracle: by simply being who we are, the world will come to fill us, to cleanse us, to baptize us, again and again.

○ *Center yourself by breathing steadily.*

○ *Bring into view one thing you are reaching for. As you exhale, reach without moving and let it open up your body.*

○ *Bring into view one thing you are needing to express. As you inhale, feel without speaking and let it open up your heart.*

Where We've Been

I have been born again and again and
each time, I have found something to
love.

—GORDON PARKS

Our ability to find something to
love, and to love again for the first
time, depends greatly on how we resolve
and integrate where we've been before.
A great model for us exists in the cham-
bered nautilus, an exquisite shell creature that lives along the ocean floor. The
nautilus is a deep-sea form of life that
inches like a soft man in a hard shell
finding his prayers along the bottom.

Over time it builds a spiral shell, but always lives in the newest chamber.

The other chambers, they say, contain a gas or liquid that helps the nautilus control its buoyancy. Even here, a mute lesson in how to use the past: live in the most recent chamber and use the others to stay afloat.

Can we, in this way, build strong chambers for our traumas: not living there, but breaking our past down till it is fluid enough to lose most of its weight? Can we internalize where we've been enough to know that we are no longer living there? When we can, life will seem lighter.

It is not by accident that the nautilus turns its slow digestion of the bottom into a body that can float. It tells us that only time can put the past in perspective, and only when the past is behind us, and not before us, can we be open enough and empty enough to truly feel what is about to happen. Only by living in the freshest chamber of the heart can we love again and again for the first time.

○ *Center yourself and close your eyes and imagine the passages that have brought you to who you are.*

○ *Inhale evenly and see which passage holds the most feeling.*

○ *Breathe steadily and ask yourself, Is the past living in me, or am I living in this passage of the past?*

○ *Do nothing today; simply be with what your heart answers.*

○ *Tomorrow, share the feeling with a friend.*

To Rest Like a Tree

Praise and blame, gain and loss, pleasure
and sorrow come and go like the wind.
To be happy, rest like a great tree in the
midst of them all.

—BUDDHA'S LITTLE INSTRUCTION BOOK

It helps to remember this. Of course,
it's hard to remember this when feeling blame, loss, or sorrow. But that's
when we need this wisdom the most.

Like everyone, I'd rather not experience the undercurrents of life, but the
challenge is not to shun them, but to

accept that over a lifetime we will have our share of them.

Avoiding the difficult aspects of living only stunts our fullness. When we do this, we are like a tree that never fully opens to the sky. And dwelling on our difficulties only prevents them from going on their way. When we do this, we are like a great tree that nets the storm in its leaves.

The storm by its nature wants to move on, and the tree's grace is that it has no hands. Our blessing and curse is to learn and relearn when to reach and hold, and when to put our hands in our pockets.

○ *Stand beside a fully grown tree. Breathe in its wisdom.*

○ *As you watch the tree stay open to wind, feel praise and blame rush you, and try to stand like the tree.*

○ *Breathe deeply, and feel gain and loss circle you and try to open your heart like a branch.*

○ *Breathe slowly, and feel pleasure and sorrow rustle your leaves and try to stand still, holding on to none of it.*

The Next Step to Health

The deeper the cry,
the more clear the choice.

I have a friend who has called into question whom he should love. This opened a field of complexities, and life quickly became an endless consideration of possibilities and allegiances.

But beneath the endless inventories, his soul was calling out from way inside, and through his pain, my friend kept hearing this far-off cry surface at the oddest times. Soon, he realized this cry was, indeed, much deeper than "Who?"

His very soul was begging to feel. This seemed more serious, more urgent, more filled with terror than a choice between one woman and another.

As he began to struggle with facing himself, my friend began to realize that all the decisions to be made about who and where and when were really heartfelt distractions from a deeper cry. Underneath all the painful ambiguities and assessments, his very soul was drowning, sinking out of reach of the feel of life. Once hearing the deeper cry within himself, his choice became extremely basic and very straightforward: How do I regain my wonder at being alive? What must I do to keep my heart from sinking?

Time and again, we are shown by the quiet courage of others that if we can let the deeper cry through, the next step to health will come plainly into view.

○ *Center yourself and bring to mind
a complex decision that needs to
be made.*

○ *Breathe slowly and try to relax
your spirit beneath the decision to
be made.*

○ *Breathe cleanly and try to let the
deeper cry through.*

○ *Feel your basic life position way
inside and admit—that is, accept
and let in—what you need to be
well.*

Birds and Ornithologists

Birds don't need ornithologists to fly.

We spend so much time wanting to be seen and named: as intelligent or good or handsome or pretty or successful or popular or as nobody's fool. Yet the spirit doesn't know it's being spiritual any more than water rushing knows it's a stream, and the heart doesn't know it's expanding with compassion any more than a hawk spreading its wings knows it's being a hawk. Nor does someone acting out of love often realize they are being kind.

From an early age, we are taught that to live fully is to be accepted, and to be accepted, we need to be seen. So we base success and even love on the effort to be seen, on how much we stand out.

However, the often painful truth we discover along the way is that to survive in an inner way that matters—that keeps us connected to all that has ever lived and is living—we sorely need to know how to be accepting.

By this I don't mean being passive. By this I mean inhabiting our capacity to see and affirm the common pulse of life we find in others, no matter how different they may seem from us.

When we do this, we no longer need to be different to be valued and no longer need to be accepted to know love. In short, we no longer need an audience to fly. We simply have to extend our sincerity to each abiding day and we will be in accord with all that is valuable.

Like flowers waiting on rain, our hearts wait on love. As much as we want to be seen and known, it is the giving of attention that keeps us awake. For giving attention opens us to love. And accepting that deep things wait like seed between us is believing in the world. So wake me by accepting me, and the world will sprout us up like grass.

○ *Be still, close your eyes, and quiet your mind until you feel the air as you breathe.*

○ *On the inbreath, open yourself to what it feels like to get attention.*

○ *On the outbreath, open yourself to what it feels like to give attention.*

○ *As you breathe, allow yourself to feel how the two merge—in and out—get and give.*

○ *As they merge, consider what it means to you to be awake.*

The Work of Love

Love courses through everything.

—FAKHRUDDIN IRAQI

I recently learned that the first form of pencil was a ball of lead. Having discovered that lead, if scratched, would leave markings, people then wrestled with chunks of the stuff in an attempt to write. Through the work of many, the chunks were eventually shaped into a useable form that could fit the hand. The discovery became a tool.

I am humbled to confess after a lifetime of relationship that love is no different. Be it a lover or a friend or a family member, the discovery of closeness appears in our life like a ball of lead—something that if wrestled with, will leave markings by which we can understand each other.

But this is only the beginning. The work of love is to shape the stuff of relationship into a tool that fits our hands. With each hardship faced, with each illusion confronted, with each trespass looked at and owned, another piece of the chunk is whittled and love begins to become a sacred tool.

When truth is held in compassionate hands, the sharpness of love becomes clear and not hurtful.

○ *Bring to mind a significant relationship that you are struggling with.*

○ As you center yourself, pray that the love you share continues to finds its form.

○ As you enter your day, stay pliable and open to becoming a tool.

Surrender Like a Duck

Beneath what I try to see
is all I need.

It was years ago, but I remember it
clearly. I was walking along the shore
of a lake in the middle of the day, and
there in the sun, a good ten yards out,
was a duck curled into itself, asleep.
With its slick tufted head tucked into
its body, it bobbed peacefully in the lapping of the water.

This little scene undid me, for here
was an ultimate lesson in trust. Without any intent or knowledge of itself,

this little duck, asleep in the womb of the world, was a deep and wordless teacher. If only I—if only we—could surrender this completely to the mystery of life, we would be carried and renewed.

It was obvious that the duck would wake and swim its little patterns on the water, but this little creature's ability to let go so completely allowed its time on Earth to be filled and saturated—if just for a few minutes—with a depth of peace that only surrender can open us to.

Only rarely have I let go this completely, yet those moments of total surrender have thoroughly changed my life. When struck with cancer, I somehow fell from the ledge of my fear and entered the operating room like this little duck. It was the threshold to the other side. When lonely and afraid to reach out,

I have somehow collapsed repeatedly into the ocean of another's love, and it has cleansed my weary heart. And in my search now for wisdom to live by, I stumble at times and surrender what I think I know, so completely, that I find myself adrift in a deeper way that is neither wise nor unwise, but simply life-affirming.

○ *When you are tired, sit quietly and breathe away the heaviness of the day.*

○ *With each breath, release a thing undone, a bruise encountered, a worry or fear that has been fed.*

○ *Do not analyze or solve these things, just breathe them away.*

○ *Once light enough, see yourself as that little duck, and feel the*

*lapping of the mystery all around
you. Feel its buoyancy.*

○ *For just ten seconds, surrender—
that is, soften all resistance—and
let the water of life carry you.*

Our Sense of Calling

Every year, around the scalp of the
planet, the caribou run the same path
of migration along the edge of the
Arctic Circle. They are born with some
innate sense that calls them to this path.
And every year, along the way, packs
of coyote wait to feed on the caribou.
And every year, despite the danger, the
caribou return and make their way.

Often nature makes difficult things
very clear. What feels like confusion is frequently our human refusal to
see things for what they are. What lesson
do the caribou shout to us with the thun-
der of their hooves as they deepen the

crown of the planet? They are evidence, even as we speak, of the fact that in every living thing there is an inner necessity that outweighs all consequence. For the caribou it is clear what it is.

For spirits carried in human form, it is a blessing and a curse that we don't always know our calling. Part of our migration is the finding out. What is it we are called to, beneath all formal ambition? The caribou tell us that, though there are risks and dangers that wait in the world, we truly have no choice but to live out what we are born with, to find and work our path.

These elegant animals bespeak a force deeper than courage, and, though some would call the caribou stupid, the mystery of their migration reveals to us the quiet, irrepressible emergence of living over hiding, of being over thinking, of participating over observing, of thriving over surviving.

In regions near the Arctic, the caribou are not just seen as animals living out an instinct at all cost. Rather, it is believed that their endless run, no matter what stands in their way, is what keeps the Earth turning. And somewhere, beneath all hesitation and despair, it is our endless call to being, in each of us and all of us together, that keeps the fire at the center of the Earth burning.

○ *Sit quietly and ask yourself what you are called to. If you don't have a sense of inner calling, please read on anyway.*

○ *Describe what arises without any conclusion. If you feel called to sing, do not conclude you need to become a singer. If you feel called to paint, do not conclude you need to become a painter. If you feel*

*called to plant, do not conclude
you need to become a gardener.*

○ *Stay with the essence of what
arises. Receive it as an energy that
lives inside you and not as a goal
you have to achieve.*

Holding in the Belly

The inward battle—against our mind,
our wounds, and the residues of the past—
is more terrible than outward battle.

—SWAMI SIVANANDA

I saw a sea otter rolling in the bay. It
held a crab or small turtle against
its belly, and on its back, it would eat
a piece, then press the crab or turtle to
its belly and turn over and swim some
more.

This stayed with me for days until I
realized that I have been living like this
otter: holding the uneaten part of my

shell to my belly as I roll through the deep, and, of course, it is impossible to swim freely while holding dead shelled things so tightly.

Indeed, trying to move on and eat the past at the same time is the cause of many ulcers. Realizing this made me stop and face the sadness of old wounds that I was holding tightly in my belly.

It made me understand, yet again, that while we try to integrate inner and outer experience, while we aspire to such a oneness, the work is often one at a time: facing ourselves without going anywhere, not nibbling at the ailing soul on the run.

○ *Still yourself and see if there is a strain between your doing and your being, a strain from tending something in your life while on the move.*

○ *If so, stop and face what is in your belly. Make what you need to tend where you are going.*

○ *Breathe deeply and let your inner and outer attention go in the same direction.*

The World Body

Earth Mother, you who are called by
a thousand names. May all remember
we are cells in your body and dance
together.

—STARHAWK

If you've ever flown, you know that
from just below the clouds, the roads
are like arteries and the cars like cells.
From above the traffic, it becomes clear
that though we all have places to go
we just keep circulating through the
streets. We race and pause and stop
and start, never sure if the road we are

turning on to will be congested or barren and free.

For example, every other day, I flip my blinker and drive down Washington Avenue. Some days, there isn't a car and the lights are all green. Other days, I have to wait, and I get irritated. But whether I'm early or late by my time, the dilation and constriction of events is something beyond my control.

In truth, like little cells, we race up and down pathways collecting and dispersing, feeling crowded then lonely, and somehow just doing so keeps the world body healthy. Like blood through a body, we are life pumping through the streets. Even waiting at a light, we are helping life go on.

○ *The next time you find yourself in a crowd, slow down and feel life circulating about you.*

○ *For the moment, let go of where you are going, and simply breathe.*

○ *Breathe out your concerns, and feel yourself as a healthy cell whose simple movement is cleansing the world body.*

WEEK 49

Hospitality

> At heart, hospitality is a helping across
> a threshold.
>
> —IVAN ILLICH

In Dante's *Divine Comedy*, Virgil lovingly guides Dante through the hell of denial and the purgatory of illusion, up to a passage of fire that Dante must cross alone, beyond which he becomes authentic. Earlier in history, Aaron guides his brother Moses off Mount Sinai back into the world, where the prophet must live what God has shown him. Even in Eden, if we can get past the punitive tellings we have heard so often, God ushers Adam and Eve to the threshold of the world, offering them the bruised and wondrous life of genuine experience that only those who are human can know.

These are deep examples of spiritual hospitality, of helping kindred spirits further into their living. Truly, the most we can ask of others is for their guidance and comfort on the way—without imposition, design, or thought of reward. This is the hospitality of relationship: for family to help us manifest who we are in the world, for friends to bring us to thresholds of realness, for loved ones to encourage us to cross barriers of our own making into moments of full aliveness.

This is the honest welcoming to table, without judgment of what we eat. Often the purpose of love is for others to guide us, without expectation or interference, as far as they can go, so that we might begin.

It reminds me of a dream I had when ill, in which I came to the edge of a forest where the narrow, lighted spaces called to me. I stood there through many opportunities till an ageless woman of great resolve appeared, saying, "You can't start, I know, and if I were kind, I'd see you halfway in, but I am more than kind. You must enter alone. I will meet you on the other side."

I'm not sure if that feminine presence was God or an angel or the peace of my own spirit, but its strong and gentle guidance was enough for me to make it through, and I never saw her again. But now, when I love by clearing paths that I and others may or may not take, I feel her in my hands.

This speaks to one of our deepest callings of love—that special hospitality for the injured, the strong action of compassion that makes it possible for those in pain to heal themselves. It calls mysteriously and arduously for the clearing of confusion and the comfort of what is real. It is the way that we who have suffered can take our turn, lifting the head of whoever has fallen, bracing their exhausted neck to drink, knowing we can never drink for them.

○ *Breathe deeply, and meditate on one act of guidance and comfort you have received that asked for nothing in return.*

○ *As you exhale, offer gratitude for that gesture of hospitality.*

○ *As you inhale, feel your own capacity for guiding without interfering. Feel your own capacity for giving comfort without needing anything in return.*

○ *As you enter your day, practice anonymous guidance by leaving a gesture of kindness or truth in the path of others. Leave half a sandwich where the homeless gather, or leave a book open to a passage of wisdom, or leave a flower on a bus seat.*

○ *Help the world by leaving a trail of who you are.*

Life in the Tank

Love, and do what thou wilt.

—SAINT AUGUSTINE

It was a curious thing. Robert had filled the bathtub and put the fish in the tub, so he could clean their tank. After he'd scrubbed the film from the small walls of their make-believe deep, he went to retrieve them.

He was astonished to find that, though they had the entire tub to swim in, they were huddled in a small area the size of their tank. There was nothing containing them, nothing holding them back. Why wouldn't they dart about freely? What had life in the tank done to their natural ability to swim?

This quiet yet stark moment stayed with us both for a long time. We couldn't help but see those little fish going nowhere but into themselves. We now had a life-in-the-tank lens on the world and wondered daily, In what ways are we like them? In what ways do we go nowhere but into ourselves? In what ways do we shrink our world so as not to feel the press of our own self-imposed captivity?

Life in the tank made me think of how we are raised at home and in school. It made me think of being told that certain jobs are not acceptable and that certain jobs are out of reach, of being schooled to live a certain way, of being trained to think that only practical things are possible, of being warned over and over that life outside the tank of our values is risky and dangerous.

I began to see just how much we were taught as children to fear life outside the tank. As a father, Robert began to question if he was preparing his children for life in the tank or life in the uncontainable world.

It makes me wonder now, in middle age, if being spontaneous and kind and curious are all parts of our natural ability to swim. Each time I hesitate to do the unplanned or unexpected, or hesitate to reach and help another, or hesitate to inquire into something I know nothing about; each time I ignore the impulse to run in the rain or to call you up just to say I love you—I wonder, am I turning on myself, swimming safely in the middle of the tub?

○ *Sit quietly until you feel thoroughly in your center.*

- *Now rise and slowly walk about the room you are in.*

- *Now walk close to the walls of your room and meditate on life in your tank.*

- *Breathe clearly and move to the doorway and meditate on the nature of what is truly possible in life.*

- *Now step through the doorway and enter your day. Step through your day and enter the world.*

At Random

Random is the instant a horse at full
speed has all four hooves off the ground.

This is the original meaning of the
word. It refers to the mystery of
unbridled passion, to the lift that results
from total immersion and surrender. In
our age, however, *random* means without design, method, or purpose. It refers
to utter chance. It helps us dismiss whatever appears to be beyond the control of
our will. If we didn't author it, it must
be accidental.

Yet our lives are full of unexpected surges of kindness that seem to come from nowhere. Just when you're thirsty, a cup is gathered and passed around. Just when you are lonely to the point of snapping that bone way inside that you show no one, someone offers you a ride or steadies the grocery bag about to drop from your grip. Just when you feel nothing can raise your sad head from the lonely road, the deer stutter across the road in exact rhythm with Handel.

So what might we learn from the horse at random? Consider how all of its energy and desire mounts from the brief moment it inhabits itself fully, and in that moment, it flies. Only to touch down again. And to fly again. And touch down again. For us, the moment at random is the moment of holding nothing back, of giving our all to whatever situation is before us. In that charged moment, we come as close to flying as human beings can— we soar briefly with a passion for life that brings everything within us to meet our daily world.

I experienced this again and again in the many hospital beds I lay flat in while going through cancer. When I could hold nothing back—not tears, not pain, not frustration or anger—I found myself at random, off the ground, though I couldn't get out of bed. And remarkably, it put me in the flow of the lives around me.

For just as pain in the body signals other cells to flood the injured area, our honest experience lived at random calls other lives to our aid. Just as blood flows from healthy parts of the body to those that are injured without either part knowing they will meet, so too in the

Universal body. We flow to each other's aid, often without knowing where we are headed. Mysteriously, the life force heals itself this way. And what we call "change" or "luck" or "coincidence" is the circulation of life healing itself through us and in us.

○ *Do one thing at random today.*

○ *If a patch of sun catches your eye, hold nothing back. Go stand in it and raise your face to the sky.*

○ *If you're caught in the rain, open yourself to it, however briefly.*

○ *If you hear live music on the street, seek it out and listen quietly for a moment.*

○ *If you see something beautiful, smile slowly. If it still seems beautiful, allow yourself to laugh that you have the privilege to see it twice.*

○ *Hold nothing back. Allow what touches you to change your path.*

In a Burst of Oneness

When wax and wick work best,
light and heat are all that's left.

Like a candle, our wick of spirit is
encased in our humanity, and when
our spirit is touched, we light up until
all we know melts and changes shape
for the burn of our experience. Repeatedly, our sweat and struggle burns our
sense of self and world away, so that
our Divine spark can be released, again
and again. These moments of Spirit-
Lighting-Up not only rearrange our
lives, but they light and warm those
who stay near.

In such moments, we become one with what we see, and this sudden One-ness is what the faithful of all paths have called Love. And in the illumination of Oneness called Love, all that's left is a willingness toward birth, an urge to be touched by something timeless and fresh. All that's left is the want of deep parts in strangers. To relish the waking over being awake, the burning over being burned, the loving over being loved.

When we can be—no matter how briefly—at one with what we have in common with all life, we are rewarded beyond attachment and ownership. This is the difference between becoming a singer and becoming the song. This is the best of ambition: that the dancer melts into the dance, and the lover melts into the act of love, and the builder melts into the thing being built, until in a burst of Oneness, dancer and lover and builder are one.

Perhaps momentarily, when swimming with the stream, we are the stream; when moving with the music, we are the music; when rocking the wounded, we are the suffering. Perhaps momentarily, when thinking without masks, we are pure thought; when believing without doubt, we are God. Perhaps love is an instrument we play for all we're worth in an orchestra yet to be convened. Perhaps this is why, in the fullest moments of loving or knowing or being, we go nameless and timeless and breathless— everything about us used up, like a candle, burned over and over, just to light entire rooms with our flicker.

○ *Watch someone doing something they love. It could be a as simple as gardening, cleaning a treasure, grooming a pet, stacking wood, or washing a child.*

○ *Observe in detail how they attend their task.*

○ *What lets you know that they love what they are doing?*

○ *Is there a moment where they seem to be one with what they love?*

○ *What can their act of loving teach you?*

ABOUT THE AUTHOR

Mark Nepo moved and inspired millions of people with his #1 *New York Times* bestseller *The Book of Awakening,* a spiritual daybook from which these weekly reflections have been taken. Beloved as a poet, teacher, and storyteller, Mark has been called "one of the finest spiritual guides of our time," "a consummate storyteller," and "an eloquent spiritual teacher." His books have been translated into more than twenty languages.

Having taught in the fields of poetry, health, and spirituality for forty years, Mark has published fourteen books and recorded eight audio projects. Recent work includes: *Reduced to Joy* (2013), *Seven Thousand Ways to Listen* which won the 2012 Books for a Better Life Award, *Staying Awake* (2012), *Holding Nothing Back* (2012), *As Far As the Heart Can See* (2011), *Finding Inner Courage* (2011), and *Surviving Has Made Me Crazy* (2007), as well as audio books of *The Book of Awakening, Finding Inner Courage,* and *As Far As the Heart Can See* (2011).

Mark has appeared with Oprah Winfrey on her *Super Soul Sunday* program on OWN TV, and has been interviewed by Oprah as part of her SIRIUS XM Radio show, *Soul Series.* He has also been interviewed by Robin Roberts on *Good Morning America* about his *New York Times* bestseller *The Book of Awakening. The Exquisite Risk* was cited by *Spirituality & Practice* as one of the Best Spiritual Books of 2005, calling it *"one* of the best books we've ever read on what it takes to live an authentic life." Mark's collected essays appear in *Unlearning Back to God: Essays on Inwardness*. Other books of poetry include *Suite for the Living* (2004), *Inhabiting Wonder* (2004), *Acre of Light* (1994), *Fire Without Witness* (1988), and *God, the Maker of the Bed, and the Painter* (1988).

As a cancer survivor, Mark devotes his writing and teaching to the journey of inner transformation and the life of relationship. In leading spiritual retreats, in working with healing and medical communities, and in his teaching as a poet, Mark's work is widely accessible and used by many. He continues to offer readings, lectures, and retreats. Please visit Mark at: *MarkNepo.com, threeintentions.com,* and *simonspeakers.com/MarkNepo*.

Based on the symbolism of the wheel, Red Wheel offers books and divination decks from a variety of traditions. We aim to provide the ideas, information, and innovative approaches to help you develop your own spiritual path.

Please visit our website to learn more about our full range of titles.

www.redwheelweiser.com